Jing Si Aphorisms

靜思小語

Contents

《談時間》

Chapter 1

TIME

時間可以造就人格，

可以成就事業，

也可以儲積功德。

Over time, we can build great character, achieve great success, and cultivate great virtue.

用智慧探討人生真義，
用毅力安排人生時間。

Use wisdom to

contemplate

the meaning of life.

Use resolve to organize

the time you are given.

「前腳走，後腳放」

意即：

昨天的事就讓它過去，

把心神專注於

今天該做的事。

As we put

the front foot down,

we lift the back foot up.

We let yesterday go,

and focus on today.

未來的是妄想，

過去的是雜念。

保護此時此刻的愛心，

謹守自己當下的本分。

The future is illusion,

the past is a memory.

Protect the love

of this moment.

Focus on

your immediate task.

生命無常，慧命永存；

愛心無涯，精神常在。

Life is impermanent,

wisdom is eternal;

the love in our heart

is boundless,

and our spirit

will always remain.

人生無常，

人命只在呼吸間，

一秒間過不了關，

生命就結束了。

所以，要好好把握

每一分、每一秒。

1

Life is impermanent.
It exists in the space
of a breath.
Life ends when the
breathing stops.
We must
cherish every moment.

未來的成就完全是在掌握分秒中造就出來，「未來」也是由「現在」累積而成。

*Our future
accomplishments
are determined entirely by
how every second in
our life is put to use.
The future
is the cumulation of
many "nows".*

《 談 慈 悲 》

Chapter 2

COMPASSION

最幸福的人生，
就是能寬容與悲憫
一切眾生的人生。

1

A person with

a generous heart

and compassion

for all beings

leads the most blessed life.

不辭勞苦的付出，便是

「慈悲」。

1

To willingly

undergo hardship

for the sake of others

is compassion.

「慈心」不能缺乏
親善的態度，

「智慧」不能缺乏
謙虛的涵養。

Being compassionate,

we are friendly and kind.

Being wise,

we are truly humble.

把貪念轉為滿足，
把滿足化作慈悲。

Transform greed into
contentment,
and contentment into
compassion

解除人間的災難，
一定要從
改善人心做起。

To end the disasters
of the world,
we must improve
the human mind.

《談謙虛》

Chapter 3

HUMILITY

即使已達智慧圓融，

更應含蓄謙虛，

像稻穗一樣，

米粒愈飽滿垂得愈低。

A wise person must be humble and unassuming, like the rice stalk that bows under the weight of ripe grain.

唯有尊重自己的人，

才能勇於縮小自己。

1

Only those
who respect themselves
have the courage
to be humble.

縮小自己，
要縮到對方的眼睛裡，
還要能嵌在對方的
心頭上。

To be humble

is to shrink our ego

until we are small enough

to enter another's eyes

and reside in

their heart and mind.

看淡自己是般若，
看重自己是執著。

To regard ourself lightly
is prajna (wisdom).
To regard ourself highly
is attachment.

不能低頭的人，

是因為一再回顧

過去的成就。

People who are

preoccupied

with past achievements

cannot humble themselves.

《 談懺悔 》

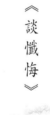

Chapter 4

REPENTANCE

人都是在原諒自己的

那一分鐘開始懈怠。

We start to slacken

the minute we find excuses

for ourself.

勇於承擔，

是一分動人的力量；

勇於承擔錯誤，

則是一種高尚的品格。

To shoulder a burden
is an inspiring force;
To admit a mistake
is a noble virtue.

大錯誤容易反省，

小習氣不易去除。

●

1

It is easy to reflect on

major mistakes.

And hard to eliminate

small bad habits.

懺悔則清淨，

清淨則能去除煩惱。

Repentance purifies

the mind;

a purified mind is

free of worry.

人最難看見的，

就是自己。

To see clearly

within ourselves

is the

most difficult thing to do.

《 談 做 事 》

Chapter 5

EFFORT

信心、毅力、勇氣
三者具備，
天下沒有做不成的事。

Nothing is impossible with confidence, perseverance, and courage.

只要肯用心去想、
用心去修、用心去做，
就沒有不能成功的事。

1

Willing to think,

cultivate ourselves,

and take mindful action,

there is nothing

we cannot achieve.

要以理來轉事，

不是拿事來轉理。

● 1

We must carry out our tasks

according to principles,

not let our principles

be compromised

by our tasks.

凡事守好自己的原則，

不要牽強應酬；

常去應酬，

往往度不到對方，

反而會被拖下水。

Abide by your principles

in everything you do.

Never act purely

to satisfy others.

For rather than

satisfying others,

you may be in

over your head.

做事要有赤子之心、
駱駝的耐力、
獅子的勇猛。

• 1

When doing any task,

have the innocence of a child,

the endurance of a camel,

and the courage of a lion.

好事，需要你、我、他
共同來成就。

所以，不要有
你、我、他的成見。

Good actions require everyone's cooperation. Let go of personal bias.

處理事情，感情要蘊藏
在理智中；
與人相處，則要把感情
表現在理智上。

●

1

In handling matters,

let your mind

influence your heart.

In dealing with people,

let your heart

influence your mind.

Chapter 6

REFINEMENT

整體的美，
在於個體的修養。

The beauty of a group lies in the refinement of its individuals.

一個人的修養、氣質，均在行、住、坐、臥四威儀中自然地顯露出來。

1

*A refined disposition
is naturally expressed
in the way a person
walks, lives, sits,
and sleeps.*

面容動作、言談舉止
合宜得體，
都是從日常生活中
修養忍辱得來。

It is through the daily cultivation of tolerance and humility that we become refined in demeanor and conduct.

欣賞他人，

即是莊嚴自己。

To appreciate others

is to dignify

ourself.

《談知足》

Chapter 7

CONTENTMENT

世間的物質
本來是為人所用，
但不知足者因欠缺智慧，
竟淪為「被物所用」。

• 1

Material objects are

meant to be used.

Yet people who lack wisdom

become discontent

and enslaved

by material objects.

人生有求即多苦！
如果只是一味地
要求他人，
會為自己招來
無窮的痛苦。

●

1

How bitter life is
when we have desires!
Our demands on others
bring endless misery.

人生若能減低欲望，
生活上便沒有什麼
值得計較！

If we can reduce our desires, there is nothing really worth getting upset about.

知足之人，雖臥地上，

猶為安樂。

不知足者，雖處天堂，

亦不稱意。

One who is content
finds great happiness
even sleeping
on the ground.
One who is discontent
will never find happiness
even in heaven.

知足的人，心量開闊；

心量開闊，對人對事就

不會計較。

One who is content

is immensely broadhearted.

A broadhearted person

will not be

in dispute with others

over any matter.

人要知福、惜福、再造福。

Realize you are blessed,
and cherish these blessings.
Then continue to cultivate
more blessings.

● 1

世間的海可以填平，
但是小小一個嘴巴，
卻永遠填不滿。

●

1

The ocean can be filled,

yet the tiny mouth

of a human being

can never be filled.

Chapter 8

LEARNING BUDDHISM

學佛的第一步
是要少欲知足，
使心靈安住，
智慧增長。

*The first step
on the path of Buddhism
is to lessen our desires
and accept what we have.
Then our minds
will relax and we begin
to gain wisdom.*

以愛待人、以慈對人，

則不惹人怨，

亦能結好緣。

When we treat others
with loving-kindness,
we will not stir up
ill feelings.
And we will be able to
form good relationships
with others.

菩薩

不是土塑木刻的形象，

真正的菩薩能做事、

能說話、能吃飯，

能尋聲救苦隨處現身。

Bodhisattvas are not idols made of wood; real Bodhisattvas are people who eat, talk, work, and relieve suffering in times of need.

人人本具菩薩心，
也具有和菩薩同等的
精神與力量。

Everyone has
a Buddha nature,
and a Bodhisattva's
strength and spirit.

經即是道，道即是路，

莫執著經典

而不肯實踐經義。

The Sutra points the Way;

the path for us to walk on.

Do not become

so attached to the Sutra

you forget to

actualize it in practice.

禮佛是為了訓練我們的恆心、耐心、清涼心，也是去除傲慢，陶冶自我身心的課程。

Prostrating to the image of Buddha strengthens our mind and body, nurtures perseverance, patience and tranquility, and eliminates arrogance.

佛法很簡單，只要去除

貪、瞋、癡三毒，

就可以明心見性。

•

1

Dharma is very simple:

eliminate greed, malice,

and ignorance,

and you will discover

your own true nature.

直心即道場。

●

1

Be faithful and honest

from deep inside,

this is the essence

of spiritual cultivation.

教法不必聽太多，

若能身體力行，

簡單的一句，

就能啟發真正的善根。

*There is no need to learn
many teachings.
If we can put one simple
verse into practice,
we can awaken
our true nature of goodness.*

《談做人》

Chapter 9

LIVING

每天都是生命中的
一張白紙，
每一個人、每一件事
都是一篇生動的文章。

Every single day of our life

is like a blank page

in our diary.

Every person we meet,

every event we participate in,

is a lively essay.

人一生的行為，

不管是善是惡，

皆由時間所累積。

● 1

The behavior of a person

during his lifetime,

be it good or evil,

is accumulated over time.

每天無所事事，
是人生的消費者；
積極付出，
才是人生的創造者。

● 1

Doing nothing
and idling time away
consumes our life.

Giving to others
with total dedication
creates our life.

什麼都沒做，

就是空過的人生；

能不斷付出利益人群，

就是大好的人生。

Life is empty
if we do nothing
to pass the days.

Life is great and wonderful
if we work unceasingly
for the betterment
of mankind.

為人處事要小心、細心，
但不要「小心眼」！

Be careful and mindful

when dealing with others,

but do not be

narrow-minded.

雙手健全
卻不肯做事的人，
等於是沒有手的人。

•

1

To have two good hands
and refuse to work
is no different than
having no hands at all.

只要能張開眼睛，

每一天

都是我的新生之日，

都是我做人的開始。

When we can wake up
and open our eyes,
each day is a birth
of new life,
a new beginning
to start our life afresh.

做人固然
不應將自我看得太重，
但也不要自輕己靈。

Do not think too highly

of yourself,

and yet,

never underestimate

your ability.

要平安，得先心安；

要心安，須先得理；

理得心安，闔家平安。

To live in peace, we must
have inner peace.
To have inner peace, we
must have a clear conscience.
When our conscience is
clear and our mind at peace,
we bring peace and bliss to
those around us.

難行能行，
難捨能捨，
難為能為，
才能昇華自我的人格。

Continue even when it is

hard to go on,

release even when it is

hard to let go,

endure even when it is

hard to bear,

this is how we build

our character.

口說好話，心想好意，
身行好事，腳走好路。

Speak good words,

have good thoughts,

do good deeds,

and walk the right path.

轉一個角度來看世界，

世界無限寬大；

換一種立場待人處事，

人事無不輕安。

*View the world
from a different perspective,
the world is vast and wide.
Change to
a different viewpoint
in your relationships and
in dealing with all matters,
and everything will be
light and easy.*

做事，一定要秉持「誠」與「正」的原則；而待人，則要用「寬」與「柔」的態度。

Be honest and truthful
in everything you do.
Be gentle and forgiving
in your relationships
with others.

人性之美，莫過於誠；

人性之貴，莫過於信。

The beauty of humanity
lies in honesty,
The value of humanity
lies in faith.

《談責任》

Chapter 10

RESPONSIBILITY

人生因為有責任

而踏實，

逃避責任

就是虛度人生。

Life becomes meaningful
when we shoulder
responsibilities.
Avoiding responsibilities
makes our life empty.

不要因貪求清閒，

而希求減輕責任；

應該增強自己的力量，

擔當更重大的責任。

Do not ask for

less responsibility

to be free and relaxed;

Ask for more strength.

與其擔心社會現狀，

不如化作信心，

並付出一分愛心。

Rather than worry about the condition of our society, why not replace it with confidence and with dedication to contribute with loving kindness?

即使自己

只是一根小螺絲釘，

也要注意

有沒有鎖上、鎖緊，

以便充分發揮功能。

Even the tiniest bolt

must be screwed on tightly

in order to perform its best.

《談逆境》

Chapter 11

ADVERSITY

碰到逆境時，

應心生感激，

這是可遇不可求啊！

In the face of adversity,

be grateful,

for such opportunities

do not come by easily.

逆境、是非來臨，

心中要持一「寬」字。

When conflict and
adversity arise,
always preserve
a spacious heart.

要原諒一個
無心傷害人的人，
不能做一個
輕易被別人傷害的人。

Forgive those

who unintentionally hurt us.

Do not be someone

who is easily hurt by others.

人在平安的時候，
很容易迷失自己。
偶爾有小挫折或坎坷，
反而能喚醒良知、
長養善根。

When life is safe and smooth,

we can easily

lose our direction.

Yet even a small

setback or misfortune

can awaken our conscience,

and nurture

the seeds of kindness.

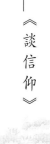

《 談 信 仰 》

Chapter 12

FAITH

人應該相信自己，

但是不可執著。

Believe in yourself,

but do not be attached

to your own point of view.

無信與迷信二者，

寧願「無信」

也不要「迷信」；

信必須智信。

*Atheism
is better than
superstition.
Faith must be guided
by wisdom.*

智信者深體佛法之精神，

迷信者曲解宗教之美意。

1

A wise believer understands the essence of Buddhism. Those who are superstitious misinterpret the virtue of religion.

人有正確的信仰，
在人生旅途走的路
就不會有差錯。

●

1

When one has true faith,

one will not go wrong

on the journey of life.

迷信就會疑心生暗鬼、

問神卜卦，

取信於籤詩、筊杯，

而無法真正深入教理。

False understanding

leads to superstition,

the search for answers from

psychics and soothsayers;

in this way,

we cannot realize

the ultimate truth

of the teachings.

人生在世，
但求一心正念，
心正氣盛，
心開運通。

We must practice
right mindfulness.
The right state of mind
strengthens us;
and a happy mind
attracts good fortune.

《 談 修 行 》

Chapter 13

SPIRITUAL PRACTICE

「修」是修心養性，

「行」是端正行為。

The process
of spiritual cultivation
is to nurture virtue
and rectify conduct
and behavior.

同道，是指同修間
若有錯誤的行為，
可彼此更正、
相互惕勵。

To walk the same path of spiritual cultivation means practitioners unite to inspire each other and reflect on weaknesses in behavior and conduct.

把專心變成一種習慣，
心不散亂就有定力。

●

1

Practice mindfulness
in your daily life.
A mind free of
wandering thoughts
develops inner strength.

人既然生在世間，
就不能離開眾緣，
修行也不能離群隱世。

*Born into this world,
we are always with people;
hence spiritual cultivation
cannot occur in isolation.*

一切言行舉止
能精神統一，
心念一致，
就是禪定。

When our spirit and actions

are in harmony;

when our heart and thoughts

are in accord,

that is deep meditation.

「戒」是不起心動念；

「定」是臨危不亂；

「慧」能運心轉境。

Precepts allow our mind
to be free from disturbance.
Equanimity allows us
to be calm under adversity.
Wisdom allows us to take
control of the mind
and change our destiny.

《談寬柔》

Chapter 14

TOLERANCE

理直要氣和，

得理要饒人。

Remain soft-spoken
and forgiving,
even when reason is
on your side.

普天之下，

沒有我不愛的人，

沒有我不信任的人，

也沒有我不原諒的人。

There is no one on this earth
I cannot love, trust,
and forgive.

對人有疑心，
就無法愛人；
對人有疑念，
就無法原諒人；
對人有疑惑，
就無法相信人。

We cannot love
when filled with suspicion.
We cannot trust
when filled with doubts.
We cannot forgive
when unwilling to believe.

多一分對他人的疑慮，

就少一分對自己的信心。

The more mistrust we feel,

the less confidence we have.

心量大福報就大。

The greater our generosity,

the greater our blessings.

忍讓可避免爭執，

柔和大愛可轉禍為福。

*Tolerance and accommodation
can prevent disputes;
Gentleness and great love
can transform disasters
into blessings.*

一個真正成功的人，
必須人人都能容得下你，
你也能容納每一個人。

A truly successful person

is accepted by everyone

and accepts everyone.

《 談 喜 捨 》

Chapter 15

JOYOUS GIVING

如何達到
生死自在的境界？
唯有靠平常多培養
「喜捨」之心，
方達提得起、
放得下之境界。

● 1

How can we be free from the suffering of birth and death? Only when we nurture our heart with joy and unselfish giving can we truly release our attachments.

捨去眼前的煩惱，

才能當下擁有

慈悲的法喜。

• 1

Let go of all worries,

only then will you appreciate

the happiness of a

compassionate heart.

捨得、捨得，
能捨才能得。

Let go of all attachment,

only then will you receive.

付出勞力又歡喜，
便叫做「喜捨」。

To give with joy

is to help others

with a happy mood.

Jing Si Aphorisms 靜思小語　❶

著 作 者	釋證嚴
美術設計	天將廣告
出 版 者	慈濟文化出版社
	臺北市忠孝東路三段217巷7弄19號
	電話：02-2783-7503
	傳真：02-2653-6114
郵政劃撥	14786031慈濟文化出版社
印 製 者	禾耕彩色印刷有限公司
出 版 日	2001年10月 初版一刷
	2002年2月 初版四十五刷
定 價	125元

感恩美國、馬來西亞慈濟人合力翻譯，
及Neil Bond協助。

ISBN 957-8300-92-1　　Printed in Taiwan